From Latchkey to Leadership

*A practical blueprint for channelling
the talents of inner city youth*

KATHY GYNGELL AND RAY LEWIS

CENTRE FOR YOUNG POLICY STUDIES
57 Tufton Street London SW1P 3QL
2006

THE AUTHORS

KATHY GYNGELL graduated from Cambridge with a First Class Honours degree in Social Anthropology, then from Oxford with an M.Phil in Sociology. She is currently the Chairman of the Addiction Working Group of the Social Justice Policy Group.

RAY LEWIS is the founder and director of Eastside Young Leaders' Academy. He is an ordained Church of England clergyman, a former prison chaplain and was a governor of Woodhill Young Offenders Institution.

Acknowledgements
Support towards research for this Study was given by the Institute for Policy Research.

The aim of the Centre for Policy Studies is to develop and promote policies that provide freedom and encouragement for individuals to pursue the aspirations they have for themselves and their families, within the security and obligations of a stable and law-abiding nation. The views expressed in our publications are, however, the sole responsibility of the authors. Contributions are chosen for their value in informing public debate and should not be taken as representing a corporate view of the CPS or of its Directors. The CPS values its independence and does not carry on activities with the intention of affecting public support for any registered political party or for candidates at election, or to influence voters in a referendum.

ISBN No. 1 905389 29 9

© Centre for Policy Studies, June 2006

Printed by 4 Print, 138 Molesey Avenue, Surrey

CONTENTS

Foreword

1. My journey   1

2. Black youth in inner city London   10

3. Eastside Young Leaders' Academy   12

4. Expanding EYLA   23

Postscript: the principles and beliefs of Ray Lewis

FOREWORD

When I first started Eastside Young Leaders' Academy my vision was to produce a generation of young men with the ambition, the character, the strength, the vision and the wisdom to make their mothers and fathers proud; young men who will take their places in the community, who will buck the statistics whereby there are more black men in prison than there are in further education. It was to find a way of producing a generation of leaders who would in turn make this country great again — because I do not believe you can have the "great" back in Britain until the black man here reaches his potential.
Ray Lewis speaking at the launch of the EYLA Mentoring programme, 25 March 2006

Eastside Young Leaders' Academy (EYLA) opened in the East End of London in November 2002. The brain child of Ray Lewis, a former governor of a Young Offenders Institute, EYLA offers a programme of mentoring, tutoring and training for black boys who are most disruptive and most at risk of school exclusion. It is designed to develop the boys personally, to teach them how to take responsibility for their future, to raise their aspirations, to harness their leadership skills and to prepare them for corporate and community leadership. It does this by providing the boys with structure and rules and by creating a commitment to learning within the context of what effectively is an extended family of adults and male mentors. Currently 60 boys are enrolled.

The aim of EYLA is to reverse the negative trends of low academic achievement, exclusion from school and criminal action

FROM LATCHKEY TO LEADERSHIP

which typify young black males in inner-city London. It admits boys who have at least one parent of African or Caribbean origin.

The Academy's programme complements the boys' normal schooling. It does not replace it. Boys on the cusp of exclusion are referred by local primary and secondary school head teachers after the commitment of the parents of the boy has been sought and gained. Activities include a weekly Saturday school, after-school tutoring, summer residential camps and community service.

The discipline at EYLA is intentionally tough. Boys wear a uniform and high attendance and punctuality are demanded at all times. A strict code of behaviour is demanded. Boys commit key lessons to memory. The presentations given by the boys show that, from the youngest to the oldest, they have gained the confidence to speak publicly and to express their ideas cogently and clearly.

After only three years, the results are remarkable.[1] The behaviour of the most intransigent boys switches from negative to positive. One teacher who visited the Academy said:

> *I am Harry's teacher. I cannot understand what has happened to him in 48 hours. Whatever you're doing here seems to be working.*

EYLA involves the boys, their families and their community and motivates all three. It provides a model of what can be done in the most deprived of communities with inspired local leadership and energy.

---

[1] Data collated from the children's schools and parents, together with an external audit undertaken in June 2005 show that there has been an 80% reduction in short-term exclusions, a 70% improvement in academic achievement and a 90% change in career plans. Only 5% of boys drop out of EYLA and 98% of parents attend the regular parent meetings. On average, each boy completes 60 hours community service a year.

FOREWORD

PROGRESS...

Martin is a handsome and bright boy who came to EYLA when he was nine years old. He had obviously been bored at school, misapplying his energy and creating his own entertainment. He challenged everything at home and at school and would never accept anything his parents or teachers told him without evidence. He wouldn't obey rules save those which he established for himself. The whole class followed his lead.

Frequently excluded from school, Martin's behaviour had become steadily more difficult and dangerous. Despite his age and lack of progress in school, he quickly learned the language and qualifications of the street. He was on the starting block of that downhill race into drugs, gangs and criminal behaviour. Martin was referred to EYLA by his head teacher and he recalls hearing the word "no" being said and meant. He discovered love and boundaries and that things like respect were non-negotiable.

Martin's change was dramatic and he is now a leader of leaders; still handsome and bright but also focussed and diligent.

His dream today, aged 12, is to win a place at Oxford University.

This is progress and typical of what happens with 95% of the children who come here

FROM LATCHKEY TO LEADERSHIP

...AND SETBACKS

Danny came to us when he was ten years old. He had already had several temporary exclusions from school and had a reputation for violence, disruption, rudeness and a long record of truancy.

At the beginning, his progress was almost too good to be true. He went from a demon to an angel in three months – it was nothing short of remarkable. His school, his mother, all of us were really pleased with how he well he was doing.

That was before his mother became ill and his absent father came back. He wasn't keen about Danny being a member of the Academy. Soon thereafter things began to go wrong. He fell in with his friends who led him down the wrong path. Due to the divisions between his parents, we couldn't do much.

He stopped coming to the Academy and his life went from bad to worse. He began taking drugs and stealing cars. He has now exhausted every community sentence that can be given to him and at just 14 he is now facing a custodial sentence. The Youth Offending Team rang me last week. "Is there anything you can do?" they asked. "Nothing" I replied. It is now too late for us to help.

I saw Danny in the street the other day. He could hardly walk as he was so high on drugs. He had been a chubby boy. Now he is as thin as a rake. He tried to avoid looking at me when I said "Danny, what has happened to you?" Soon he will be in custody from which he will come out worse. He will be dangerous. God knows what damage he will now inflict both on others and himself.

FOREWORD

EYLA works in the London Borough of Newham in partnership with local schools and the business community. It has won corporate support, gifts in kind and goodwill from a number of well-known companies and enterprises.

EYLA is expensive. It costs £4,000 to £5,000 a year for each boy – roughly the same as the cost of full-time state school education. It currently receives the bulk of its funding from charitable grants. Only 1% of its budget is currently met by the Local Education Authority (although Newham LEA is considering paying substantially more in recognition of EYLA's success in turning round difficult children). Yet while it may be expensive in the short term, it also provides real value for money: it is far cheaper than the cost of a pupil referral unit (which is estimated to be around four times the cost of mainstream education).[2] It also provides intensive tutorial support throughout the year as well as a wide range of holiday programmes. It is also far cheaper than keeping a man in prison – a realistic possibility for those difficult children who do not go to EYLA. This is now estimated at £37,300, a figure which excludes the cost to the victim of the crimes committed, the police work involved, the judicial system, the probation services, and the youth justice and youth offending teams before and after sentence.[3]

EYLA is a remarkable success story. It is the result of the hard work and inspiration of a remarkable man. What is even more extraordinary is that Ray Lewis has created a model which, if copied carefully, can work under the direction of focused local social entrepreneurs and community leaders throughout the country. This paper shows how dozens of Young Leaders' Academies can be opened – on a franchise basis – across the UK following the winning formula devised by Ray Lewis.

---

[2] A pupil referral unit is a local authority school that has been specially organised to provide education for children at risk of exclusion.
[3] See Prison Reform Trust, *Prison Fact File*, May 2005. Data for 2003/04.

FROM LATCHKEY TO LEADERSHIP

A rule of thumb is that while 80% of new businesses fail after five years, 80% of franchised businesses succeed. If that ratio holds true in the world of social entrepreneurship, then in the near future we can expect to see Young Leaders' Academies opening in other London boroughs and in the other great cities of the UK. As with all franchises, the franchisees will have to show great commitment, will need great energy and will face many challenges. It will not be easy. They will have to be enterprising in raising funds, dealing with local authority bureaucracy, managing their staff, creating a clear ethos and maintaining discipline. Some will fail. But those who try will also have one great advantage: that they will be doing something which has been proven to work.

For the sad truth is that the need for similar institutions is widespread. The DfES says that 9,880 children were permanently excluded from schools in 2003/04, and a further 202,000 children had one or more "fixed-period" exclusions. About £450 million a year is spent on helping difficult children.[4] Evaluation of the Government's costly Behaviour Improvement Programme (140 teams targeting difficult schools) suggests that it has had only limited impact in improving attendance and no impact on exam results.[5] It begs the question of whether centrally administered and externally imposed interventions in schools with pupils and their

---

[4] See Hansard, 9 May 2006, Column 158W in which Jim Knight MP (Minister of State, Department for Education and Skills) stated that in 2005/06 local authorities in England spent £12.8 million on excluded pupils; £227.8 million on Pupil Referral Units; £84.8 million on Behaviour Support Services; £5.0 million on Behaviour Support Plans; £47.8 million on Support for Inclusion; and £67 million for Special Education Needs administration, assessment and co-ordination. These figures do not include the cost of Special Education Needs itself which is substantial.

[5] See DfES, *Research and Evaluation of the Behaviour Improvement Programmes*, 2005. This also stated that while schools in the Behaviour Improvement Programme had a reduction in fixed period exclusions, they also had a small but significant increase in permanent exclusions.

FOREWORD

families, however well-intentioned and apparently thought out, is the route to follow or is the best way to invest scarce resources.

Too many young children in our country today have been failed by their schools, by their parents and by the environment in which they have been brought up. What Ray Lewis has shown is that, with the right framework, and within the community environment, this pattern of failure can be reversed. These children can be helped.

If you want to contribute to this venture, please see the appeal at the end of this pamphlet. Or if you would like to take the first step in becoming an Associate Leadership Director, then write to Ray Lewis, Eastside Young Leaders' Academy, PO Box 23703, London, E7 0YR.

Kathy Gyngell
June 2006

CHAPTER ONE

MY JOURNEY

I have no inclination to analyse dysfunctional behaviour. I recall Martin Luther King who spoke of "the paralysis of analysis". If I had a hundred boys and intervened in the same way, some would probably still end up in prison. Having said that I am sure beyond reasonable doubt that if one intervenes early, one intervenes effectively and one intervenes intelligently, one can make a difference.

I AM THE THIRD CHILD OF FOUR, born in Guyana in 1963. I came to England in December of that year as a nine month old baby so I know of little else but England. Like many children of West Indian families at that time we were gathered around the major railway stations and underground networks because that was where the work was. My father worked as a porter for British Rail and my mother had successive factory jobs over the years. Unfortunately, but like so many of our contemporaries, my mother and father split up. I was about five or six and from then on my mother raised us in his absence and without the support of the Child Support Agency or any other agency that could force money out of him. He showed little interest in our upbringing save for the occasional Christmas card.

There were four of us then, my two older brothers and my younger sister brought up in one room in Brixton by a single mum in dubious circumstances. I am aware at first hand of the pitfalls and perils of being a single parent without the support of the extended family. Mum worked long hours leaving me to raise my younger sister.

FROM LATCHKEY TO LEADERSHIP

We would lie about our dad's whereabouts and tell stories that he was away on an oil rig and such. We were poor but we got by.

My mother was quite strict, but because of the number of hours she worked, supervision was not a possibility. For the most part we had to be responsible for ourselves and each other. It is difficult enough for nuclear families to raise children. In the absence of a father, it is very difficult for a woman on her own to make a man out of her son. So a vacuum is created. As a full-time working black woman, it was hard enough for her to fulfil her own role as mother. So a vacuum was created. As growing boys struggling with the physiology of adolescence, the reality was that we learnt our rites of passage on the streets. We learnt about adult life as children.

In our then modern flats and high-rise buildings, we had to learn to fight and to fight well at a very early age. I was regularly beaten up at the very large all-boys comprehensive school I went to in Vauxhall. It was very tough; my dinner money was stolen every single day without let up. Mum was at work but even if we were able to communicate with her, we still had to protect ourselves. You had to develop survival tactics. Bullying was commonplace and my dinner money was stolen on a regular basis.

I was involved in my own share of petty crime. Everybody was the same. It was, literally, the survival of the fittest.

The first break in my life came when my mother remarried and moved us to Walthamstow. Life in this part of London seemed less pressurised, the language less violent. Expectations were higher and I was forced to address my own behaviour especially in school. Making that adjustment was hard. I just transferred my behaviour from one school to another and became the dominant force. It took me a couple of years to adapt and I nearly did not make it. It was so very different to where I had been before. The school was much smaller in numbers and the children were much less aggressive. So I was the bad boy, constantly in trouble and excluded. I was the usual suspect.

MY JOURNEY

Renewal

I got the hang of it in the end for one reason alone. It was because one teacher believed in me. This woman, Miss Archer, said to me, "Ray, no one else in the year group wants you but I am willing to take you and I'm going to take you because I believe in you".

That was the beginning of a new reign. I was about 13. From that day on, my life changed. I believed I could accomplish something in school. By the time I left I had some O-levels and a couple of A-levels under my belt.

Although I came out of school having done quite well and wanted to go to University my mother said it was out of the question: there was no money. My stepfather delivered furniture but my mother had begun working for the civil service after she remarried. I saw that for her it had made a difference. So for five years after leaving school in 1981 I worked as a civil servant, following in mum's footsteps as the only example I had. Although I gained a couple of promotions it was a dead end. I found the work soul-destroying and boring.

But I did have other good fortune. I met a lovely girl, Pam, just one year after leaving school, in 1982, and we married in 1984.

She was two or three years older than me and worked as a teacher. Meeting her gave me my first positive example of black family life. Her parents were together. They lived in a very nice house. Her father worked while her mother was a home-maker. They ate at the same table, said prayers before meals and I felt like a fraud sitting there the first time. I didn't know what to do. I had never eaten at a table before. My family had eaten in front of the TV at different times, never together. I remember that first time feeling quite hot and embarrassed. This was new for me – almost alien. However my image of family life then changed.

Pam was also my example of spirituality. As a regular churchgoer and keen Christian she got me involved in church youth activities several times a week after work. This was my only solace to my monotonous day job.

FROM LATCHKEY TO LEADERSHIP

Our vicar, John Pearce, began mentoring me one-to-one and introduced me to the deeper aspects of Christian philosophy. In 1987, I applied to Oakhill, an Anglican theological college in North London, to take a degree in theology. Then three years later I was ordained and took a curacy in Islington and later became a clergyman in Newham.

I was a great reader and through working with young people I became much more socially aware. It was during this period I got involved in prison work. These were the two things of particular concern and passion for me. I began to work part time as a Chaplain in Brixton prison. It was fascinating. And even though it was in my spare time I loved it and it took hold of me. Going into prisons and working with the kind of people you meet in these places, I could not get enough of it. The other thing I cared about was having our church full of youngsters. I would bring them in off the streets and that didn't always go down well. As far as I was concerned that was the kind of ministry and expression that I wanted but it was not possible within the confines of the expectations of parishioners and other clerics. This was too much for me as I am prone to the odd bad word and telling things as it is; and that just won't do as a clergyman. So while I realised that my reverence for God was profound, the way in which I expressed myself and wanted to go about things was not quite the way that others wanted me to.

So Pam and I decided to look abroad for renewal and to meet our need for a challenge. We went to the Caribbean island of Grenada where I was a clergyman and had the responsibility of looking after a number of schools. It was a tough call and nearly burnt us out.

Coming back to Britain in 1999, we had to decide what I would do. Did we want to go back into parish life or not? We were agonising over this when I bumped into a friend who told me that the prison service was looking to fast-track governors. He said, "Ray, I know it's not on the chaplaincy side but you might be even more effective".

And that is how I got into working with young offenders.

MY JOURNEY

Becoming a Governor

For the fast-track process, they sent me round lots of prisons. I was put on a residential course for three months and then became a governor of a young offenders institution, Woodhill, in Milton Keynes.

Woodhill had been built in 1992 and looked like a University. It was modern, clean with individual cells with their own toilets. Most had television. Cells were designed to house one person but with the increase in the number of people being incarcerated were routinely used for two.

The age range of inmates was 17 to 21 and the total prison population was about 700; smaller than Feltham, 1000, and bigger than Aylesbury, 500. First-time offenders were housed alongside those with a great deal of prison experience.

From my experience eight out of ten of these boys were involved in drugs in some way or another on arrival. Cannabis was not even on the register! Nine out of ten would arrive, dealing, using, and pushing. Most of them had a habit. They were stealing and such like to fuel their habit. Drugs play a huge part in the lives of youngsters nowadays – it is like a rite of passage. Many thousands experiment and some get hooked. Others still get involved in drugs at a criminal level.

It is well known in prison culture that little to no one is guilty. Many prisoners feel like the victim including sex offenders. The whole of society is reflected in the prison population, young, old, rich, poor, sick, sad and every racial group. There are however more black youths in custody than in university. For many this was their university, a place of higher learning with the greatest honours bestowed upon the studious.

The kind of prison reception that greets a prisoner has nothing to do with a blonde behind a desk. It begins with a strip search. They look up your anus, they look round your testicles, they look round your mouth, they run their fingers through your hair. You are basically subjected to 15 minutes of indignity. That is when we take away your identity, your liberty, your dignity and your privacy. Most suicides occur that first night – certainly in terms of attempts – when you have been searched and you have been escorted to your cell by an Alsatian dog. You are put in a cell and the door is shut. Then reality dawns. A lot of them look for a quick way out. So you are always very mindful of young men at that particular stage. I always watched them.

There are other things that go with prison. Your name goes for a number. You become a statistic. Your identity therefore is no longer the same. Your privacy has gone. That is punishment. Now whether that is enough or not, I don't know. When you ask a young man what he misses most, the first thing he will tell you is the door handle. The ability to turn that door handle and be free to go whenever you want. This and the intense feeling of just being shut in sometimes for 20 hours or more; all this begins to take effect on your soul and begins to take effect on your mental health one way or another.

The absence of hope

The most debilitating things that I ever came across was the absence of hope. Young men with huge potential, just doing nothing. I am no liberal. If you have done wrong, you need to be punished. Whether or not prison serves its role very well in terms of rehabilitation, society still needs a break from people who have committed serious offences. But if one hangs around a prison for long enough, you can't help but sympathise with the people you are caring for. The sentence is the punishment. You are not sent to prison for more punishment. So my job and the prison officers' job is not to put upon the prisoner further than what a judge hands down.

Prison staff often ask themselves the question, "who is it who is in prison?" You can almost feel imprisoned yourself even though you sleep in your own bed. As with many occupations, the prison service has its own powerful sub-culture, fuelled by low pay and a common enemy. Staff showing sympathy or any other helpful attitude toward inmates are sneered at by their colleagues. After a season one can become no better than those committed to you by the courts.

MY JOURNEY

Working in such an oppressive environment meant that prayer became something even more important to me than before. Without being able to strengthen myself, I would have collapsed. It was depressing.

There are opportunities in prison for education and for courses of rehabilitation but they depend on whether there is enough staff available for supervision. Half the time, there isn't. Prison officers carry the highest sickness rates of any profession in the country. The stress levels are enormous. So at any one time the prison was probably carrying a sickness absence of around 20% and sometimes up to 30% or 40%. Then the only option was to lock down a wing. So instead of going to an art class or for an airing a young man will find himself banged up and not allowed out for 24 hours at a stretch. In many prisons, each cell has its own toilet the practice of slopping out has gone for the most part. Showers are available only twice weekly unless you are an enhanced prisoner. You get used to the smell after a while because that part of your brain goes to sleep.

When a young man has spent the last four Christmases behind bars, it is hard to find hope that he can hang on to. When his little sister is growing up and his mother is going grey in his absence; when he knows the indignity she suffers of being searched whenever she visits him, her breasts felt and dogs sniffing at her private parts in order to ascertain whether she is carrying drugs; when a young man knows that his mum has just gone through that, it is enough to cut him up.

A defining moment for me occurred in Christmas, 2000. We had allowed families of the young offenders in for the Christmas service and I sat in the Chapel with a few of them afterwards – just ordinary people. For one or two of them this was the first time in a prison. It was clear that until then their view on prisons had been "lock them up and throw away the key". That was until *their* son ended up behind bars. But that Christmas day I realised that they too were doing a prison sentence. I spoke with them for ages and all their stories were the same. Their boy had not done well at school – he couldn't listen, he wouldn't do as he was told. The Social Services had intervened and they had tried this and that. The stories were not of a blow-out, but of a slow leak. Alarm bells went off in my head. It was a moment of clarity for me. It came to me that if we can identify a child early we have a much better chance of doing something about it.

It was that thought of the 'if only' arising from speaking to mums, dads and carers that made me look back at my own family life; coming from difficult circumstances, I knew what they were talking about. If I had turned left instead of right, if Mr Patel had looked up instead of down when I was nicking the Smarties then maybe my road would have been different. If I had been half a stone heavier when running off and hadn't been able to get up and over the wall – maybe I would have been caught too... and then what?

But why had their lives so inevitably followed the wrong track? The answer that came to me was simple. It was because no one was there for them. It made me realise when I spoke to these people that I was not in a position to judge. But it led me to thinking again: is there something else I can do?

Epiphany

It was not uncommon for me to work 14 hours a day and in view of this my wife and I had an agreement that we would have lunch together twice a week at home as the jail was just five minutes away. It was so close to home that I could take my walkie-talkie home and still hear it.

On one such occasion Pam ushered me in with great haste. Instead of our usual salutations she impressed upon me the importance of watching the Oprah Winfrey Show. Oprah was interviewing Kirt Bennett, Director of the Young Leaders' Academy, in Baton Rouge, America. This Academy had just won a presidential award. My wife said to me – these were her words – she said: "Ray isn't this what you have been talking about for so long?"

MY JOURNEY

Within two weeks I found myself in Baton Rouge in the company of Mr Bennett and his staff.

For the next two weeks I researched and enquired. I spoke to parents, teachers, board members and young leaders. What I learnt and experienced is that where there is a will, there is a way. Arguably the issues of social exclusion are greater for the black male in the US than here in the UK. Levels of poverty, opportunities for crime, peer pressure, family factors all seem more acute in the richest nation in the world. And yet to witness 200 plus young black males standing to attention in a gymnasium, fire in their eyes, self-controlled, focussed and hopeful was a life-changing experience. At last I had found what I was looking for.

I returned to Britain and immediately resigned my post, plundered my savings, put the children on rations and began the work of establishing a Young Leaders' Academy in the UK.

CHAPTER TWO

BLACK YOUTH IN INNER CITY LONDON

> *I took 12 children away for the weekend, and we were having some honest talks, these twelve, thirteen and fourteen year olds who were becoming men and wanting to learn about that. I said, "Well, let's look around this room. Including myself there are thirteen of us. How many of us grew up with a father in the home?" What I meant by that, the guy who was there originally, is he still there at the end? One boy put his hand up. And that's about the average statistic – one in ten, one in eleven. There are no males in our households.*

SOME OF OUR CHILDREN are very, very damaged. There are almost as many reasons as there are children – sexual abuse, drugs the cloud of depression that hangs around poor communities, a host of things. Talking to mothers, just looking at them is enough to explain why their sons are in such a state. They are burdened with debt. They are desperate. Some are at their wits end.

We chose Newham to site the Academy because it is one of the most racially mixed boroughs in Europe. 21% of the Newham population is black African or Afro-Caribbean. A careful look at this social mix reveals why we targeted black boys. Statistically they are doing far worse than any other racial group. This includes boys of dual ethnicity and they often have some of the worst personal identity problems and conflicts to deal with in a community like this.

Alongside this multiracial diversity, Newham also has the highest percentage of lone-parent families with dependent children in the country. This number has more than doubled since 1991. Newham has seen high levels of inward migration and on the Government's 2004 Index of Multiple Deprivation, it ranked as the fourth most deprived borough in London, eleventh in England and Wales, 23 of its 24 wards falling in the 10% most deprived in the country.

The educational indices show similar problems. We have the highest proportion of our population between 16 and 74 without any qualifications at all of any borough in London. 13% of the children have a special needs statement. In 2003/4 Newham's rate of permanent school exclusions was well above the national average. Few black boys stay on at secondary school. And Newham is also well above the London average for offences per thousand of the 10 to 17 year old population.

The police confirm what I see everyday: that family factors such as poor parental supervision and discipline, family conflict and parental attitudes that condone anti-social and criminal behaviour, are common amongst "problem" young people in the borough. A culture that equates manhood with immediate gratification, guns and drugs is manifest. It explains much of the deprivation of aspiration and achievement and is exactly what Eastside Young Leaders' Academy is here to combat.

CHAPTER THREE

EASTSIDE YOUNG LEADERS' ACADEMY

Joe was the most disruptive child in his junior school, his influence undermined the running of the school. All the other children looked up to him. His teacher, said if she could get Joe to work, then the whole school would work. If Joe would not co-operate then she could do nothing. So Joe came to us. We have been asked by the head teacher: "what have you done to this child? He's transformed".

THE ETHOS OF EYLA is that children are born in a family, but raised in a village. I happen to be one of the village chiefs. But the business of education belongs to all of us. And the important thing that we want to create in this village is consistency for the child.

Get in early
The consensus among teachers and youth workers is that to make progress and change lives one must intervene early. We all agree that when they get to the teenage years things are almost set in stone. Our first principle is to intervene early.

Prevention has got to be better than cure from both a moral and economic perspective. If we can identify them at eight years old and stay with them through their teenage years, what we can do, with fewer resources, is to save lives. It is however more than just prevention. It is an investment in their future and in society's future.

Prevention is a pathway to progress. In the stories you hear from the children if you just give them a little time, you see the effects of your intervention in wonderful ways.

EASTSIDE YOUNG LEADERS' ACADEMY

Selection

We ask: "Does he smash any windows? Has he beaten up teachers? No? Well then, we're not interested." Our job is not to analyse their delinquency, which may be to do with self-esteem, frustration or a whole host of things. Our job is to find the solutions, to be able to channel their energies positively.

EYLA is a specialist intervention service. We are not here for any black boy. We are here for those who would most benefit from the programme. My experience as a prison governor, my experience as a father, my experience of working with youths is that, very often, the most disruptive children are those with innate leadership gifts. So it is the foul-mouthed, the aggressive, the violent, the drug-users, the ones who have had brushes with the law, stealing cars – these are our candidates.

Children are going to school from increasingly difficult backgrounds and circumstances. They display difficult behaviour and their schools are at a loss to know how to manage it. When a child is told off, he tells his parents, and then the parents are aggressive towards the teacher. They are often violent. So the school is in a no-win situation.

By contrast, the Academy is different. Number one, we are clear from the outset about our expectations and standards. Number two, we expect our parents to work with us, otherwise it won't work at all. Without such principles, schools are fighting a battle that they are going to lose.

We're in a state of crisis. The reality is that many of our boys will be going to prison. Don't forget that what we're dealing with here is a generation of boys who could not care less about God or man. They have no fear, they have no inhibitions, and they have no conscience. Lying, to my boys, to my young leaders when they arrive, is as natural as blinking. For these boys, theft is what you do when you want something. The idea of paying for it never crosses their minds.

FROM LATCHKEY TO LEADERSHIP

When these children come to us, 90% will have experience of stealing, smoking, inappropriate sexual behaviour and the like. Where have they learnt it? From the streets, along the council rise corridors, behind the bins and the like. For the most part if one challenges their thinking, one can affect their values. A recent conversation I had with a group of boys on sex, and their attitudes towards sex, turned when I said to them: "you've all got sisters, haven't you? Yes? How do you fancy someone talking about your sister like you do about other girls? How would that feel to you?" Well, that arrested their attention. "What about your mum? If I said, "Mum, come and give me head" – how would you feel about that?" For the first time, they had the paradigm shifted and it worked.

Violence is something that many of the children enjoy. What we teach at the Academy is, "let's consider another way". To do that, we have to do it forcefully, radically and we do it with an air of urgency. Some people feel that we are boot camp-like in our mentality. I have never run a boot camp so I don't know. What I know is that people come here voluntarily and the boys enjoy being here. For the first time in their lives, somebody loves them and has set boundaries for them. The boys come and find me every day when I'm around to tell me what they've done, what they're up to, what their day's been like. For these boys, to take them away for a weekend, as I do, is just staggering. I take them out of Newham to a restaurant, and say, "what would you like?" This is a new experience for them. "Can I choose *anything*?" they ask. "Yes. You can choose anything". And then, to be able to get them to really talk about themselves, I say: "This is a sacred place, what's spoken here stays here." Is that a boot camp?

On one occasion one boy said, "Sir, I don't know who my dad is, but I'm beginning to feel as though I need him". Everyone was silent. Another boy said, "well, I do know who my dad is but I wish I didn't because he takes drugs, and I've seen him do it and he makes my mum take drugs."

EASTSIDE YOUNG LEADERS' ACADEMY

Conditions

We follow a clear and unchanging admissions procedure. A boy's school faxes me a registration form telling me why they feel the child needs to come here, the issues that he is facing and his predicted grades. Then we arrange a meeting with the parent or carer.

A condition of joining the academy is that the child has to have a parent or a guardian who will be in regular touch with the Academy. When I first see a group of parents who are interested in enrolling their child, I try to dissuade them from sending their child to the Academy. I suggest they try to find something else for their son because I make it clear that this is hard work, a great deal of hard work. It's like the Grand National. You start off with 36 runners and riders, and by the time you get to Beacher's Brook, there's two left. We make it very hard to get in. If we just opened the doors, then we would have had 3,000 children through here in just two years. And that is just in Newham.

We tell them you have to abide by the rules and that you have to pay your fees. We charge on a sliding scale from three pounds a session to a pound. Everybody can pay something. *Everyone,* because we feel it is an important part of their own learning process. It also gives them ownership, knowing that they are buying into something. People don't respect what they don't own.

If a parent will not work with us, we will not take that child. If the child is in care, and the foster parents or local authority will not act *in loco parentis* we won't take the child.

We also keep emphasising just how bad things are. I say to parents, "Your son is two laps behind in a three lap race. There is no time for politics, apologies or pontificating." Finally I'll challenge them and say no one can make the decision tonight, you go home. Call me in the cold light of day and let me know if you want your child to be part of this Academy.

The only thing we make easy for the child and his family is that we transport them from their school to the Academy and then from the Academy to home. This we believe is important. It ensures the child's presence and safety.

FROM LATCHKEY TO LEADERSHIP

Urgency

In the Academy I instil a sense of urgency. All the boys feel that. Many are far behind academically and have got to catch up. That catching up process is important because I want them to learn from it, so they never go back there again. They have to understand the graft that's got to be put in. It works because the boys are very keen to please us.

When a child joins the Academy, he has a session with the Counsellor who gives him a brief induction and finds out about him. She then briefs the core staff and alerts them to any sensitive subjects for the child. We all get a feeling of who the child is and what his needs are. Between myself, Anne, the Project Manager, and Delores, the Education Manager, we will take them through who we are, what we do and why.

Each child has a personal development plan with a quarterly review. It is vital to understand clearly each child's academic needs and to build a programme that is suitable for that child. Our education manager looks at each child and plans their curriculum and assigns them to a tutor. Sometimes it's one to one, one to four usually, one to six, exceptionally. And the tutors sit with these children, work is set, graded and marked, commented on, and sent back to me, a summary version. And then we map the child's progress.

Values

All the boys get to know my seven Rs. We all know about the three Rs, reading, writing and arithmetic but in addition to that, we teach the importance of responsibility, respect, reason and rites. Our values, what we believe in, are to be seen all over the academy.

The boys have to recite them and memorise these. Woe betide them if they turn up to the academy and are unable to recite them, that will be 20 push-ups. They learn that they are *responsible* for their actions, that they *respect* all adults and their peers. They learn that when they walk through the door they are supposed to hold it open for the next person. We also teach the importance of *reason*, that anything presented to them is to be thought about and digested, not just swallowed.

Finally, *'rites'*. That is to say, we teach the boys something about purpose. Why are you on the planet? Of all the sperm that left your father's testicles and yours was the one... *you* – why you? If they can get a sense of their own uniqueness and purpose for their lives, they will gain a sense of direction. "I am fearfully and wonderfully made", said Jeremiah, "you knew me even before I was in the womb". I want them to appreciate that they count for something.

Thinking positively

I want the children to dream dreams and have visions. We encourage them to aim for the top because the bottom is overcrowded. But they have to own these aspirations and my business is to foster this ownership.

Our task at the Academy is to provide the children with sufficient exposure and experience to light the touch paper of their aspirations.

Sadly, so many children do not rise beyond the poverty of their own parents' aspirations.

We don't believe in children at risk; we believe that every child was born to succeed. It is not to say that everybody is going to be a rocket scientist, not at all. You can sweep the streets and still be a respectable, honourable man. It is how you do what you do – it's how you do it, how you carry yourself. Now it may be humble, it may not be very much, but if you do it to the best of your ability, that is what we expect.

So these are some of the values we instil in our youngsters, and particularly about their life purpose. You are here for a reason, and once you've sowed that seed in their heads, it goes a long way. They keep coming back to me.

FROM LATCHKEY TO LEADERSHIP

The quarterly review

A key part of the structure of expectations placed around each boy at the Academy is the Quarterly Review Process.

The meetings are chaired by the Project Manager, Anne. They are set up for each boy on a quarterly basis to review his progress. The meeting will last up to one and half hours. Present will be the boy, his parent, usually his mother, sometimes his main school teacher (from the school he goes to) and our education manager.

The school gives us feedback from a monitoring form that we require them to complete. This details the boy's grades, his attendance record, his effort, his homework completion and his general behaviour. We will also review his community service contribution, which must be at least four hours per month. His mother has to report back on his behaviour at home and tell us of any domestic issues, past or ongoing and the boy himself has to write his own report of how he sees his progress. Each meeting begins from reviewing whether the boy has met or exceeded the targets which were agreed at the previous meeting. We do tick boxes but the atmosphere of the review is normally pretty informal.

Educating the family

Our teachers visit the boy's home once a fortnight at least. My staff may tell me that they've never seen a book in their home, lots of magazines and CDs but no books. We encourage parents to read. We ask them: "are you members of the library? Why not as a family have a visit, once a month, to the library? Take books out yourself then your son sees you reading and that legitimises the exercise." I say to them there's no point telling your son to read when you are watching Eastenders or whatever. I say, no, that's not good enough.

They must get to know that the business of education is serious. And what we also do – and this is a voluntary thing – is to refer or find people who can help the parents read if necessary. Because some of our parents find it difficult – and we acknowledge that.

EASTSIDE YOUNG LEADERS' ACADEMY

Often what goes on here goes straight back home. Everything that we teach our boys, we teach at home, with the exception of some of the social skills. For example, we teach our boys etiquette, how to eat properly and so on. But we won't teach the parents that necessarily. Iron a shirt, shaking hands, how to look somebody in the eye. We don't teach parents that kind of thing, but we tell them that we're doing it with their sons. Our ethos is we will work with boys and their families as best we can, in order to get the best for them. But though their circumstances may be lowly and their children may be doing poorly, our aim is to do our best to equip them to raise their children. We cannot substitute for the parents. We do not and must not take away from them their responsibility to raise their children. It is theirs. We reinforce, we support, we supplement, we complement. But we do not do it for them.

Discipline

We have a clear policy about discipline. Discipline is not the same as punishment. The latter aids the former. Discipline is internal. We expect our students to be self-disciplined as it is not the tutor's role to manage behaviour. His or her job is to teach. If a student is behaving badly, our tutors will simply refer him to the staff responsible for keeping order.

Both parents and boys learn that what we threaten we carry out. Some boys are startled to hear for the first time the word "no". Others sense and respect that there is something within us that will not compromise or give in. We establish clear boundaries at the very beginning. And children quickly get to know what their boundaries are.

When they arrive, difficult and out of hand I say, "I have a bigger ego than all of you put together". I say to them, "I'm rationally crazy. My word is law – this is not a democracy." But I also make it clear that if they work and co-operate with me, we'll have fun. If they do not, they will not have fun.

One example of this principle was when we were taking a group of 35 to 40 boys to spend a day at Butlins. One of the youths decided to play up. There and then we cancelled the trip. Everyone suffered. But not as much as the person who caused the trip to be cancelled. He was extremely unpopular. *He* confessed everything. But it was too late, the coach had gone. But everybody learned from that day, it's been a living legacy. "Don't do it" they say, "because Mr Lewis doesn't mess about. He means it". And so they live with that burden and have understood the idea of what letting the team down means.

We set standards the boys must meet. Every boy who comes to the Academy becomes a member of the 100 Club. He starts off with 100 points. Every time he is late, if he's absent without reason, for example, five points will be deducted. They learn that you can only retrieve points, not by good behaviour – that is expected – but by exceptional behaviour, by doing additional community work for example. Each child is expected to maintain an average mark of 90 by the end of the term. If he does not, he forfeits his trips, he can't go on outings.

Once every two weeks, they are given out the cards with their scores on and some close their eyes before they open them, praying.

I often have to explain to parents that our practices give me no joy but I cannot make an exception. "If I do that, your child will not learn", I tell them. I explain that life seldom gives you a second chance. This sanction is not about missing a trip.

What I'm trying to teach the boys here is not just about "do well in the academy and impress me." It's how to develop the life skills that will take them beyond their peers.

It is interesting that every parent comes to appreciate the rules too when their child forfeits his rewards. I have had parents in tears. I had two boys, brothers who had accumulated enough points for a weekend away. They had to be in a certain place by half past nine. At 25 to ten, they weren't there. We left. The mother sent a text asking please let me know the route you're taking. I switched off the phone. These boys have never been late again. The mother said, "Ray, they were devastated, they gave me hell all weekend," she said, "I felt as if I was grounded". Another boy was supposed to come on a weekend. But we were not able to get parental permission. Why not? Because she had changed her phone number and hadn't told us. So, the boy came that Saturday, he brought his things, but I said, "well, you can't go, I needed your mother's permission and I didn't get it by the Friday deadline." She sent me a letter, apologising, and she said, "Ray, I feel as if I'm in the dock. I will never, as long as I live let him down again." I said, "Well, we've all learnt then".

I say to the mothers that one of the things they will hear from their son, is "when I become a man, I put away childish things". I tell them "You're an adult; you also need to put away childish things – you have children." Now many of our parents don't know how to do this, they still want to be childish, because perhaps they never had a chance when they were children.

I always teach my boys what we call the pilot's code, whatever you do in life, remember the pilot's code: in God we trust, everything else we check. I say, "if you keep that in your mind, you won't go far wrong".

Mentoring – why it is so important
Our boys need black male role models. That is why for this Academy the Director must be black. Our teachers are male and female. Our counsellor is female. They all give guidance, love and attention. What these boys need are examples they can follow. In March 2005 we officially launched our mentoring programme, inviting black adult males in the community, men who might be friends, relatives, co-workers to train, to act as a role model, guide, compatriot or challenger, one for each individual boy at the Academy.

In some parts of the world teenagers don't exist. They are just young adults in waiting. Here in the West we have a generation without moorings. If wise men do not initiate these young men in the making, the culture of the streets will. A young man at a certain age needs to be harnessed, challenged in the right ways and given certain responsibilities. In the home where there is no dad, who is going to do it? We have to guide their parents too because they have forgotten what they went though as children. What's more they have forgotten that they have forgotten. They simply don't know what to do. They are in a state of crisis and they don't know where to turn for help. They think that is how it is, how it is meant to be; that it's inevitable.

This crisis of youth in our country is made worse by a Government whose response to teenage drinking is to extend the licensing hours, whose response to the problem with drugs is to legalise cannabis and whose response to the problem with underage pregnancy is to give out condoms. No one says hang on a minute this is wrong. That word has disappeared from our language. People have picked this up and they say "well if *they* say it's all right, it must be OK for me."

The Government does all that it ought not, interfering where it ought not but not interfering where it ought. In this cauldron, people are exploiting, being exploited and left unprotected. Mothers who don't realise that having a guy in her bedroom next to her son's and that crying out ecstasy in the middle of the night for him to hear, is not helping him; mothers who don't realise that for their nine year old son to be watching the TV in his bedroom after 2am – with all that is shown at that time – is entirely wrong. Mothers who have no idea of what is appropriate and who do not realise that the TV is not the baby sitter. These people are being mugged and duped.

Corruption moves in. Drugs, crime and worse beckon to the boys. They enter a way of life that will take a counsellor 15 years to decode or reprogramme from their mind.

Parents are failing to parent. Family life has collapsed. That is the challenge facing not just EYLA but anyone else who really wants to help the children who are being betrayed across the country.

CHAPTER FOUR

EXPANDING EYLA

> *Starting up EYLA was a matter of finding the right people, getting local authority support, drafting a business plan, getting charitable support, the support of the local Chamber of Commerce, of schools, of parents, through conferences, presentations and publicity. It wasn't easy and we made mistakes. But we know what we are doing now. And there is no reason why others can't do it as well.*

THE LESSONS LEARNT IN SETTING UP EYLA can be applied elsewhere. EYLA has already had several requests to replicate its winning formula and is now in a position to help suitable individuals set up their own Young Leadership Academies on a franchise basis.

Associate Leadership Directors
The crucial feature of a successful Leaders' Academy is a leader; someone to whom the boys can look, relate and respond. Whatever processes or structures are in place, central to the organisation is the personality of the leader. The successful franchising of EYLA is predicated on the finding and training of entrepreneurial leaders to become Associate Leadership Directors who in due course will lead their own Academies.

Ray Lewis and the Education Director will be responsible for all aspects of the training of Associate Leadership Directors. It is expected that it will take one year to train and put in place Associate Leadership Directors (although this will vary according to the experience and qualities of the applicants). This training will involve:

FROM LATCHKEY TO LEADERSHIP

- a part-time secondment with EYLA in Newham gaining practical hands-on experience of day-to-day management issues, learning on the job, facing real-life issues and resolving them under the tutelage of experienced EYLA staff and the young leaders themselves;

- building support in the host community, developing partnerships, fund-raising, planning and putting in place the foundations for the new Academy. EYLA will visit the host communities with the Associate Leadership Director and give presentations to the local authority, schools, potential donors and partners and other local organisations;

- theoretical and academic tutorials (probably in partnership with the YMCA, George Williams College);

- relationship support and mentoring from Ray Lewis.

The programme is intended to ensure a successful transfer of the core values, culture and understanding to the Associate Leadership Directors; and to ensure that the necessary infrastructure in the host communities will be in place.

The Management Team
At the start-up, the following positions will need to be filled: the Associate Leadership Director; a full-time Project Manager/Administrator with financial and regulatory responsibilities; one part-time teacher; and two part-time leadership instructors.

The Board
Each franchise will have its own Board of Directors. Directors must be leading figures mainly drawn from the host community and be selected in conjunction with EYLA. The Board will have the principal responsibility for the franchise and legal accountability for its operations. It will supervise and support the Associate Leadership Director, ensure the financial solvency and accountability of the organisation, represent the franchise in the

EXPANDING EYLA

host community and be the final arbiter in disputes. It is expected that the Board will meet on a quarterly basis. The Board will also be responsible for setting the salary of the Associate Leadership Director. Board members will have significant management or professional experience.[6]

Autonomy
Subject to a suitable Board being put in place, each franchise will be largely autonomous. Local initiative and responsiveness is essential and must not be stifled by an over-bureaucratic or regulatory approach. It is hoped, however, that there will be open communication between franchisees so that ideas and best practice are shared with all Academies.

Timetable
It is envisaged that three Academies will be opened in the first phase. These Academies are likely to be situated in London. Once these Academies are operating successfully, then applications from further franchisees will be considered.

EYLA will be committed to the continuing support, supervision and monitoring of all the new Academies.

Programme costs
EYLA intends to approach potential donors to meet the start-up costs for the first phase. The principal cost will be instituting the training programme and supporting the Associate Leadership Directors during the start-up.

---

[6]   The EYLA Board comprises of Steven Norris (Chair); Francis Maude MP; Clifford Herbertson (Group Business Development Director, Exel); Stanley Musesengwa (Chief Operating Officer, Tate & Lyle); Fitzroy Andrew (Head of Diversity, Post Office); Dawn Ferdinand (a Head Teacher) and Geoffrey Eze (Treasurer). Its patrons are Dr John Sentamu, Archbishop of York, and Rudolph Walker (actor and playwright).

FROM LATCHKEY TO LEADERSHIP

A check list for Associate Leadership Directors

The following list outlines the issues which a potential Associate Leadership Director will need to consider during their training programme.

- Identify the needs of the host community. In Newham there was a clear need for help for black boys. In another area, the drive might be to meet the needs of a different ethnic, gender or social group.

- Become a charity.

- Prepare a business plan.

- Put together the right team with the right leadership, co-opting locally based professionals.

- Gain the support and blessing of the local MP and other prominent members of the community.

- Recruit your board. Board members must be individuals of recognisably high calibre and expertise. They should not be friends. EYLA will advise on candidates' suitability.

- Win the approval and endorsement of the Local Education Authority. The key individuals are likely to be the Director of Education and the Head of Children's services. It may in time be an important source of funding.

- Get endorsements from relevant high profile individuals. From the outset, EYLA was backed by people such as Archbishop Sentamu (who was Bishop of Stepney at the time) and Steven Norris.

- Decide your role models. The children will need to identify with someone who has successfully overcome the problems they face.

EXPANDING EYLA

- Approach potential donors. Consider asking professional fundraisers to help. It is expensive to run an Academy – but EYLA can help with ideas and endorsements.

- Seek government grants and enlist local businesses to support the Academy. Commitments can be in the form of financial investment or the donation of goods and professional services. Local Chamber of Commerce support can be accessed through "the social responsibility and diversity agenda" programme.

- Start talking to the local schools. This is where your children will come from.

- Develop a publicity strategy. EYLA's initial press release attracted great interest not least because the "leadership" focus offered a new approach to underachievement of black boys.

- Understand that the Academy must become a focal point of the community. Plan Community events. Invite local and national figures to them.

- Find simple but appropriate premises (of about 1,000 square feet). EYLA is in an old primary school building which is no longer used by the LEA.[7]

- Establish all compliance procedures. Contact Ofsted and the LEA. As the children at EYLA are all over eight years old, EYLA has to meet the Local Authority standards for Child Care. Let everyone know what you are doing.

- Get going – start up small if need be.

---

[7] EYLA's current premises are about 2600 square feet. This is large enough to accommodate up to 240 children. A new start-up would not need this much space.

AN APPEAL TO SUPPORT THE WORK OF RAY LEWIS

EYLA is a charity and is supported mainly by donations. To make a contribution, please send a cheque made payable to EYLA, c/o The Centre for Policy Studies, 57 Tufton Street, London SW1P 3QL with a covering note mentioning this pamphlet.

If you give through Gift Aid, EYLA will be able to reclaim 22% in tax.

DO YOU WANT TO BECOME AN ASSOCIATE LEADERSHIP DIRECTOR?

Starting up an Academy will require individuals with initiative, vision, enterprise and enthusiasm. They will have a forceful personality and will be people who get things done.

Running an Academy will require a real understanding of children and young adults, real-life experience of the problems of the inner city and endless reserves of patience, determination and courage.

The salary will be based on what each Associate Leadership Director has raised from the host community and will be determined by EYLA. It is unlikely to be more than £25,000 a year. The real rewards are seeing the difference you can make to a young man's life.

If you would like to be considered as a potential Associate Leadership Director, please write to Ray Lewis, Eastside Young Leaders' Academy, PO Box 23703, London, E7 0YR.

PREVIOUSLY PUBLISHED BY THE CYPS

NO MAN'S LAND: *how Britain's inner city young are being failed*
Shaun Bailey

In this searing dispatch from one of Britain's most deprived inner-city estates, Shaun Bailey describes a deepening spiral of broken families, drugs and violent crime.

Today, he works on the same estates as where he was born, trying to save disaffected neglected children, the rootless, the crack-addicted from a life of death and despair.

This highly acclaimed report describes how the problems are getting deeper every year. He tells of the gangs who are making life intolerable for many; of how drugs and alcohol abuse among the very young are leading to addiction, crime and social collapse. Of how failure and a poverty of aspiration have become engrained into the soul of the community. What, he asks, can be done?

First, the liberal consensus must be challenged. Easy access to, and liberal attitudes towards, drugs, alcohol, pop culture, teenage sex, greed, single parenthood and the celebration of violence are causing deep damage. Shaun Bailey argues that on the estates people need rules. They need to raise their expectations and to accept that their actions have consequences.

Second, they need practical help. Shaun Bailey describes how he and his colleagues have brought round heavy crack-users; how they have set up drug rehabilitation schemes, job clubs and football clubs for the young people on the estates; and of how these – and not government initiatives – are beginning to fill the void that is at the root of so many young people's problems.

"Mr Bailey... argues convincingly that Britain's inner city young need rules and moral guidelines. They also need role models who provide a clear link between hard work and success, not a culture of celebrity and bling... What they do not need is misguided liberalism" – leading article in *The Sunday Times*

THE CENTRE FOR YOUNG POLICY STUDIES

The Centre for Young Policy Studies has been set up as a subsidiary of the Centre for Policy Studies. It studies the problems facing the young (children and young adults), particularly the underprivileged young; and it aims to put forward methods of alleviating these problems.

The CPS has carried out much work in recent years in highlighting the importance to children – and to society as a whole – of family stability. Yet the fact remains that millions of young people will grow up outside a stable two parent family. Alternative support structures – predominantly voluntary – are urgently needed for these young people. Otherwise we will continue to waste their talent, destroy lives and impose great burdens on our police, prisons and social services.

The CYPS publishes papers, hold seminars and seeks to influence the debate on the young, the future of our nation, in any way it can.

Please contact us if you would like to contribute to this debate.

John Nash
Chairman
The Centre for Young Policy Studies
57 Tufton Street
London SW1P 3QL

POSTSCRIPT

THE PRINCIPLES AND BELIEFS OF RAY LEWIS

Early identification and intervention makes prevention a real possibility.

The most disruptive children are those with innate leadership gifts.

Children are born in a family, but raised in a village. I happen to be one of the village chiefs. But the business of education belongs to all of us. And the important thing is consistency for the child.

"No" means "No."

Often, for the first time in their lives, somebody loves them and has set boundaries for them.

The seven Rs. We all know about the three R's, the reading, writing and arithmetic but we also teach the importance of responsibility, respect, reason, and rites. The boys learn that they are responsible for their actions, that they respect all adults and their peers. We also teach the importance of reason, that anything presented to them is to be thought about and digested, not just swallowed. Finally, 'rites'.

In some parts of the world teenagers don't exist. They are just simply young adults in waiting. In the West we have created a generation without moorings. If wise men do not initiate young men in the making, the culture of the streets will. A young man at a certain age needs to be harnessed, challenged in the right ways and given certain responsibilities. In the home where there is no dad, who is going to do it?

In the absence of a father, it is very difficult for a woman on her own in the inner city to make a man out of her son.

This crisis of youth in our country is made worse by a Government whose response to teenage drinking is to extend the licensing hours, whose response to the problem with drugs is to legalise cannabis and whose response to the problem with underage pregnancy is to give out condoms.

The Government does all that it ought not, interfering where it ought not but not interfering where it ought.

Parents are failing to parent. Family life has collapsed. That is the challenge facing not just EYLA but anyone else who really wants to help the children who are being betrayed across the country.